SHADOWS
of My
Heart

By Virginia Glenham

**INTERNATIONAL DISTRIBUTOR
UNITED, INC.**
P.O. Box 18646
Charlotte, North Carolina 28218
(704) 536-3214

First Printing: September, 1993

Dedication

To the Glory of God,
To all of my family still living
and
In memory of my husband, daughter
and other loved ones whose shadows
are forever tugging at my heartstrings.

Cover and Illustrations by
TOM HARTMAN

Typesetting by
BEVERLY MILLER

Shadows of My Heart
by Virginia Glenham
Copyright ©1993

Library of Congress
Catalog Number: 93-86240
ISBN 1-88310-303-7
Printed in the USA

Published by Jerry Stokes
P.O. Box 18646
Charlotte, North Carolina 28218
(704) 536-3214

Direct inquiries and/or orders
to the above address.

Publisher's Cataloging in Publication
(Prepared by Quality Books Inc.)

Glenham, Virginia Barefoot,
  Shadows of my heart / Virginia Barefoot Glenham.
  p. cm.
  ISBN 1-88310-303-7

  I. Title.

PS3557.L464S53 1993   811'.54
                             QB193-21569

My heart
has a
permanent residence
for the shadows
of my mind
Shadows
of people and places
~ hence ~
Shadows
they left behind
Often they dance
right out of the past
to lighten
and brighten my day
Oh, what delightful
memories are cast
when the shadows
come out
to play

Virginia Glasham

Forword

Almost everyone can look back to one special teacher who played a significant part in shaping their lives. Mine happened to me in the form of Miss Hunter, fourth grade, Johnson Street School, High Point, North Carolina. Until then, school was an uncomfortable place for me to be.

It just so happened that she was passing by my desk when I was scribbling my first little verse. She read it to herself and then to all the children:

> I had a little pet
> The cutest I'd seen yet
> It was a little cat
> That ate a poison rat
> It died after that
> And that was the end
> Of my little pet.

She praised my efforts and encouraged all the children to do the same. After that, my imagination knew no bounds. I wrote poems about everything I could think of — my mother, mosquitos, God, whatever came to mind. Maybe some of them improved as I grew older. I have always enjoyed writing special birthday wishes to friends and family. When my husband went to war, it was an outlet for me to pour out my loneliness.

Now, with five children, eleven grandchildren, and five great grandchildren, I guess I could stay busy forever just keeping up with them. Instead, I write when the inspiration hits me — sometimes in the middle of the night when my mind is so busy that I cannot sleep.

I enjoy writing for others if they have someone special in mind and can give me the thoughts that they would like to project. I love the challenge and the sharing with others.

Index

SHADOWS
of My
Heart

SHADOWS of Inspiration 9
In His Shadow

SHADOWS of Feelings 29
On My Mind

SHADOWS of Family 47
From My Heart

SHADOWS of The War Years 67
Lost Time

SHADOWS of Young Love 79
Dreams and Things

SHADOWS of School Days.................................... 85
Flickering Shadows

SHADOWS of Cigarettes 105
Lights Out!

SHADOWS

of

Inspiration

In His Shadow

A Prayer

Most Holy Father, help me to see
The gifts that You have implanted in me.
You've created each person with such tender care,
And bestowed on us talents You want us to share;
But, we bury those talents with one excuse —
We don't have time to put them to use!
No time to call someone to brighten their day,
No time to visit — yet, we find time to play;
No time to listen to some troubled soul,
No time to remember someone who's grown old.
Please help me to place in priority
The things that are of value to Thee.
Help me become more keenly aware
Of the bountiful gifts You want me to share.

by Virginia Glenham

11

The Masterpiece

There is a magnificent picture
    Framed in my window pane;
It's background is ever changing —
    It never remains the same.

'Tis a proud and ornate steeple
    Reaching high into the sky
Bringing hope and peace and comfort
    To all the passers-by.

From sunrise until sunset
    One can see the most beautiful hues,
The clouds that drift above it
    Set in lovely shades of blues.

The sky is not always cheerful —
    Often it's cloudy or grey,
But I feel a strange excitement
    Each time I look that way!

While the steeple itself is a masterpiece
    Made of man's design,
The sky has a special artist
    Whose perfection is sublime.

by Virginia Glenham
1979

Never Too Old

You're never too old to appreciate the touch
    Of a loving hug when you need it so much!
Never too old to smell the flowers
    Never too old to recount the hours
Of precious moments in memory,
    Reliving the days that used to be;
Never too old to let others know
    That your love is with them wherever they go.
You may not see well, or perhaps cannot hear
    The birds and their singing but you know they are there.
You're never too old to feel the warmth of the sun
    Or to welcome sweet rest when the day is done;
Never too old to enjoy children at play,
    Or the comfort received when we find time to pray;
And no matter how dreary some days may seem,
    We find that we're never too old to dream.
Our days here are numbered, but Lo and Behold!
    We'll live in a land where we'll never grow old.

by Virginia Glenham

Halfway

I was reading a story the other day
About a little boy wanting to be met halfway.
The way seemed hard — going on and on
From school to home if walking alone.
"It's not so far, Mother, and I don't get tired
When we walk together, side by side."
So his loving mother would meet him halfway
And hand in hand they were happy and gay;
'Though she started out tired and feeling tested
When they arrived home she felt content and rested.
And I thought to myself, How nice it would be
To have someone always waiting for me.
Just to meet me halfway when the going gets rough —
Someone who is caring would be enough.
Then I thought of the friends both far and near
And I realized how often they are standing here
Ready to reach out and clasp my hand
Wanting me to know they understand;
And my heart filled with joy just to know they would say
"You won't be alone — I'll meet you halfway."

by Virginia Glenham

On His Time

We are like little children,

We want our way "right now";

We think God can wave His magic hand

Without rationalizing the "why" and "how".

Of course, we don't always get our way,

So we think God doesn't hear us.

We try to force our ways instead

Not realizing that He stays near us.

In desperation we begin to doubt,

We wallow in our fears

Not knowing that His answer

May take weeks, or months or years.

Then when the perfect answer comes,

We look back in awe and find

He has been preparing all the way

For that perfection — *In His Time!*

by Virginia Glenham
May 20, 1993

Do You Know Somebody's Mother?

Somebody's mother is not here today
Because she's old and feeble and grey
And her own dear daughter is far away;
    Do you know somebody's mother?

Somebody's mother is in a nursing home,
She feels deserted, sad and alone,
She's never even called to the telephone;
    Do you know somebody's mother?

Somebody's mother sets the table for one
With nothing to do when the dishes are done
But recall when the house was full of frolic and fun;
    Do you know somebody's mother?

Then there's a lady you're bound to know
Who never had the child she wanted so;
One she could talk with — Some place to go;
    She wishes she was somebody's mother.

As we think of our blessings here today,
Let's reach out in some very special way;
Write, call or visit — and certainly pray
    For God's blessings on somebody's mother!

by Virginia Glenham
April, 1985

Gift of Love

Each day we are starting our lives anew
    If we only have the wisdom to know it,
And love is around us and in us
    If we realize and take time to show it.

And God's love is so overwhelming,
    His glory is hard to behold;
For, of every second of love we give Him —
    He gives back ten million-fold!

by Virginia Glenham
1980

God's Presence

I can't think of Nature
　　Without thinking about God;
Each trail that I follow
　　I know His feet have trod.
Each breeze that comes blowing
　　Caresses my face,
Bringing joy of His Presence,
　　His Love and His Grace.
A glorious sunrise
　　Promises me light;
The soft rays of sunset —
　　Rest and peace through the night.
The storms from the ocean
　　With it's mighty roar
Show His Might and His Power —
　　And sweet calm when it's o'er.
The seasons are symbolic
　　To everyone's life
From new birth in the Springtime
　　To Winter's deep strife.
Spring showers, His blessings,
　　Blooming flowers, His Love,
A promise fulfilled
　　Is the rainbow above.
A symphony of music
　　From all the birds singing
Is profoundly more stirring
　　Than all the bells ringing.
But there is a sadness
　　That overwhelms me -
The raindrops are tears
　　He is shedding for me!

Father, you give me
　　The stars in the sky;
Father, forgive me
　　For making You cry!

by Virginia Glenham
October 11, 1989

Think About It

When you're speaking of someone
    Is it kind? Is it true?
Is it something you'd want someone
    To say about you?
Is it necessary to repeat what you've heard,
    Blaming the origin on an innocent bird?
Do you add your own version;
    Your listener, the same,
'Til it's out of proportion
    Except for the name?
How cruel, how thoughtless — this game we play,
    Never knowing the consequence of the foundation we lay.
Is it to build our own ego,
    Or to get special attention?
Or for other reasons,
    Too numerous to mention?
Others needlessly suffer;
    Sometimes, often fail
Because into some heart
    We have driven a nail.
Our Saviour loved us so much;
    He would never accuse us
Of our many sins —
    Nor would His words abuse us.

Lord, help us to think
    Only kindly of others;
Let Your love flow through us
    To our sisters and brothers.
And in speaking, say good things
    Always keeping in mind
Are our words necessary?
    Are they true? Are they kind?

by Virginia Glenham
1990

Christ Is Here!

I saw Christ today
    upon the face of a child
    All purity and innocent,
    so sweet, so fair, so mild.
And my heart swelled with the reality
That Christ is here — He's here with me!

I heard Christ today
    in the anthem and the prayer;
    'Twas in the pastor's sermon;
    I felt His presence there.
And my heart joined in the rhapsody
My Saviour's here — He's here with me!

What blessed assurance in the thought
That Christ is here today
In everything I see and hear
In each turn of the way.

What joy to have this knowledge
Not ever to question, "How".
I don't have to wait for Heaven
My Lord is with me now!

by Virginia Glenham

18

What More Love

What more love
  Than to let His only begotten son
  Die on a cross that victory over death could be won—   What more love!

What more love
  Than creating the beauty that surrounds us
  Earth, sun, stars and moon—such beauty astounds us—   What more love!

What more love
  Than taking those who are terminally ill
  Into His arms so no more pain they will feel —   What more love!

What more love
  Than forgiving all our sins and transgressions
  When we truly repent and make our confessions —   What more love!

What more love
  Than giving us ministers to teach the great story
  Of Christ and His coming again in His glory —   What more love!

What more love
  That, as unworthy as we are, choosing you and me
  To spread His love so that others may see —   What more love!

What more love
  Than sending His Holy Spirit to direct us
  And angels unaware always there to protect us —   What more love!

Thank you, dear Father,
  For Your love that never ends
  But is shown to us daily through
  Our loved ones and friends!   What more love!

by Virginia Glenham
December 1991

19

Teddy

Teddy Stallard was not interested in school,
He had a glassy unfocused stare,
His clothes were wrinkled and musty
And he never combed his hair.
When Miss Thompson graded papers
'Though she thought she loved all the same,
She got a distinctive pleasure
In marking "F's" beside his name.
Of course, she knew more about him
Than she wanted to admit:

> 1st grade showed Teddy had promise
>   but his home life was unfit;
> 2nd grade read he could do better
>   and that his mother was seriously ill,
> 3rd grade showed him a slow learner —
>   a good boy — but too serious still.
> 4th grade reported him well behaved
>   and that his mother had died;
> 4th With a disinterested father, his grades were low
>   No matter how hard he tried.

When Christmas came, the children brought gifts
Which they piled on their teacher's desk;
One read, "To Miss Thompson from Teddy"
Wrapped in brown paper among the rest,
When she opened her present from Teddy,
There were giggles all over the room —
A gaudy rhinestone bracelet
And a half bottle of cheap perfume.
She quickly silenced the children,
She held her wrist up high
"Doesn't this smell lovely?" — and they agreed
As they slowly passed her by.

With holiday anticipation, all the children fled
Except for Teddy who came to her desk
And very softly said,
"I'm glad you liked my presents;
You smell just like my mother.
The bracelet looks pretty on you, too."
(Those gifts — more precious than any other.)
When Teddy had left, she got down on her knees
With a heartfelt prayer, "Lord, forgive me, please."

More ...

When school resumed, she felt like new
Teaching the children as God intended her to.
Especially the slow ones — especially Teddy
At the end of the year for sixth grade he was ready.

She didn't hear from him 'til a few years had passed,
Then a note came — "graduated 2nd in class."
His words were few but made the tears flow,
"Miss Thompson, I just wanted you to know."

Four years later another note came
Signed, "With Love," above his name.
He graduated first at the university
"Just wanted you to know — you mean so much to me."

Then four years later his letter read,
"As of today, I am Teddy Stallard, M.D.," it said.
I'm getting married, and I'm so excited —
You are the first one to be invited.
I'd like you to sit where my mother would —
    were she here.
You're my only family — Dad died last year.
Love — Teddy.

Miss Thompson went to his wedding
With a heart filled with pride
For one of her children
And his beautiful bride!

A story put into verse
by Virginia Glenham
March 28, 1993

A Lesson Learned

Once there was a little girl
Who had such an imagination,
That she could never tell the truth
Without making it a great sensation.

One day she told her daddy
There was a lion under the tree.
When he looked out the window,
A dog was all he could see.

He said, "Go to your room and pray
And ask God to pardon you."
When she came back, she told him,
"God thought it was a lion, too."

So in order to teach her a lesson,
He gave her a hammer and nail;
Each time she told a story
She had to drive one in the rail.

It wasn't long before the fence
Had nails for all to see;
He told her when she told the truth,
She could pull one nail free.

She saw that where each nail came out
A hole where it was driven,
She would always see the wrong she'd done
Even tho' she was forgiven.

The lesson is, when you've said false things,
No matter how sorry you are,
Although you may want to take them back,
There will always be a scar.

by Virginia Glenham

Story of a Bad Boy

Once upon a time, there was a lively little boy
And doing lots of wrong things became his greatest joy!
You know what he did? — it was such a waste —
SQUEEZED OUT OF THE TUBE ALL THE TOOTHPASTE!

And that's not all ... he climbed up in the tree —
THREW DOWN ALL THE APPLES — TWO HUNDRED AND THREE!
And just as though THAT wasn't enough —
He cut ALL the hair off his little cat, "Puff."

That's when his mother came onto the scene,
And instead of scolding him for being so mean,
She said that she wouldn't be anywhere 'round him
"'Til he put things back just the way he had found them!

Now, what's more impossible? ... Can you put TOOTHPASTE back?
Or an apple on a tree — with a string or a tack?
And, oh, how messy! To put hair on a cat!
He became really sorry about all of that!

So his mother told him as best she could
That she would forgive him — for, of course, she would!
"But when you do bad things — the LESSON is true:
THOSE ARE THE THINGS YOU CAN NEVER UNDO!

Made into verse by
Virginia Glenham

Once Upon A Time . . .

He was a hard-working husband and father
    Who loved his family very much;
That's why his mind was so absorbed
    He hardly felt her timid touch.
Tomorrow would be an important day
    For a business presentation;
It meant a lot to their future lives
    Not to break his concentration.
When his little girl shied up to him
    He didn't take time to look,
She was wanting him to read to her
    From her new green-colored book.
"But Mommy said you probably would."
    He said, "I don't see how.
Go tell Mommy to read to you
    'Cause I'm too busy now."
"Mommy's upstairs — she's busy, too
    Can't you read one story to me?
And, Daddy, here's a picture
    I 'specially want you to see."
"Oh yes, Sweetheart, that picture's great,
    But I do have work to do;
Perhaps tomorrow I'll have some time
    To read your book to you."
She stood in silence for awhile
    Then decided to try once more,
But he only mumbled and nodded
    So she laid it on the floor.
"I'll leave it here to read to yourself
    Whenever you are ready,
Only read it loud so I can hear,
    You'll remember, won't you, Daddy?"

More ...

"Sure — later . . ." he now remembered
    How he'd turned his daughter away;
He imagined the touch of her little hand
    And heard her softly say,
"Just read it to yourself
    But loud enough for me to hear."
He picked the book from the scattered toys
    Among her playthings near
The green-colored book was dog-eared and torn
    For it was no longer new;
It opened to a lovely page
    That special picture to view.
His lips moved stiffly with anguish,
    His eyes were filled with tears,
No longer did he think of the careful plans
    He'd made for their future years.
For a little while he even forgot
    His bitterness and hate
For the now-jailed drunken driver
    Who had plunged through their garden gate.
He didn't even notice his wife
    Who was waiting for him to go
To the funeral home where his daughter lay
    He started reading soft and slow
"Once upon a time there was a little girl
    Who was so beautiful and fair
That the birds in the forest forgot to sing
    Whenever she was there.
And there came a day . . ." he read to himself
    But with a tinge of fear
As he lifted his head and read out loud
    Hoping maybe she would hear,
"ONCE UPON A TIME THERE WAS A LITTLE GIRL
    WHO WAS SO BEAUTIFUL AND FAIR . . . . ."

A story put into verse
by Virginia Glenham

The Christian Tree

The Christian Tree must not be bare;
   God's Holy Love is nourished there.
With warm arms reaching to embrace
   Each tiny leaf that takes it's place.

It's shade will help the weary rest,
   It's fruit will be the very best
To feed the hungry souls who yearn
   To know God's word and His concern.

Each tiny leaf — though small may be
   Adds to the beauty of the tree;
No, the Christian Tree must not be bare;
   God's Holy Love is nourished there!

by Virginia Glenham
August, 1984

The Sign

Blue ribbons for Jesus,
The sweet baby boy
Born as the Christ Child
To bring peace and joy;
Born as our Savior
To give God's salvation
To all who receive Him —
Each country — each nation;
Born to be crucified
For us on a cross
That our sins be forgiven —
Our lives, not a loss.

Dear Jesus, please help us
Show our love for you;
In all hearts this Christmas
May the ribbons be blue!

And this shall be a sign unto you —
Ye shall find the babe..........

by Virginia Glenham

26

Long Ago and For Today

The verses that I memorized
    While at my mother's knee,
I now have come to realize
    Mean everything to me.

They seem to always come to mind
    When I am in dispair,
And I feel new joy and comfort
    In my Heavenly Father's care.

The days when I learned those verses
    Are long ago and far away,
But the beauty of their lessons
    Long ago were for today!

by Virginia Glenham
1980

One wonders how far a child's mind can go,
What pathways his thoughts have trod;
My five-year-old saw our new pastor and asked,
"Can I go up and shake hands with God?"

by Virginia Glenham
August, 1987

Putting God First

When we have plenty of water
　　It's hard to imagine thirst;
When everything is going well
　　It's hard to put God first.

But what if the well runs dry
　　Or when rain doesn't fall
Or our dreams collapse around us
　　God is the first one we call.

Oh, if we would only live in His love
　　Though many of our dreams might burst,
God always promises the rainbow
　　Whenever we put God first.

by Virginia B. Glenham

SHADOWS

of

Feelings

On My Mind

Feelings

Dear Lord,

I feel that I am floating on air
    Just waiting for You to light me somewhere;
I'm aimless and listless and time seems so slow;
    Please send a fast cloud and make the wind blow!

*   *   *

Yesterday was a special gift,
    Everything right from beginning to end,
The new green earth, the sun so bright,
    And running into an old dear friend!

*   *   *

The clouds drifting by were so far away,
    And my dreams riding on them
Were meant for today!

by Virginia Glenham
1983

Symbolism

A brisk, cold wind — and the tree is bare,
Losing it's brown — once golden hair;
Now, knotted limbs are twisting there —
    Symbolizing death.

Before too long — when Spring is here,
New life in bud-form will appear,
Then a shining leaf with it's dewey tear —
    Symbolizing birth.

by Virginia Glenham
Winter, 1980

31

Drifting

Drifting in and out each day
And off to sleep at night,
Suspended into nothingness,
No goal — no spark — no light;
The emptiness — the loneliness —
The pain — the loss — the sorrow —
Yet hearts go right on beating
Today — tonight — tomorrow.

by Virginia Glenham

Contemplation

Suddenly the tree is bare,
It's leaves receding — making it bald
Except for the bird nest for it's hair,
(and the reminiscence of a sweet bird call.)

by Virginia Glenham
Winter, 1980

Intangibles

Some people have a lot of "nerve,"
Some have a lot of "gall;"
I hear some say they have a "mind,"
Some say they have a "ball."
Now, let me say I have a "chance"
Since it's near Valentine
To say — if you don't have a "heart,"
Here — take mine!

by Virginia Glenham
February, 1981

32

Pathetic Clown

Whenever I am feeling down
    I always try to be a clown;
I never want the world to see
    The sadness deep inside of me.

My clown is one who wears a smile;
    Folks think he's happy all the while;
But when alone down through the years
    His face gets smudged with all my tears.

My clown is fickle, not much fun,
    But then when all is said and done
I know the reason — know I cried
    For all the thousand dreams that died.

by Virginia Glenham

The Rocking Chair

This is a magic rocking chair;
It's power can take you anywhere;
You only need to close your eyes
To travel the land, the seas, the skies.
You can even re-live where you've already been;
Just confide in your chair the where and the when.
Your ship will come in from wherever you dock her;
Just remember, and never go off your rocker!

by Virginia Glenham

Tall and Small

"It must be wonderful to be so tall
You can reach a high shelf, or look over a wall,"
    I said this to myself long years ago,
    But there was so much I didn't know!

Now, 'twould be wonderful to be tiny and small
To be so close to the beauty of all
    The green earth — the flowers you can reach
out and touch,
    And look up to the people who love you so much!

by Virginia Glenham

A Do-It-Yourself Present

What can I give you that I made myself?
An afghan — or ceramic to place on a shelf?
Jams or jellies wouldn't last very long;
    If I were a composer, I'd write you a song.
Oh, I know what I can do!
    I can make a wish — a wish just for you!
It will be big and pretty and hold lots of things
Like pebbles and flowers and butterfly wings.
Perhaps I'll throw in a sunset or two
And top it off with a dream come true.
I mustn't forget to put in a prayer
That wherever you are, God will be there.
Really it's easy — nothing much to it —
But making a wish — I KNOW I CAN DO IT!

by Virginia Glenham

Memory's Album

My mind has a picture album;
I love to turn it's pages,
Pictures of favorite people
I've known all through the ages.

They never grow old, I remember each one
The way they used to be;
What joy, what fun we always have
In my mind's memory!

It's so exciting to go back in time,
To feel pretty and to be young again,
To play in the Winter's beautiful snow,
Or behold how Spring has sprung again!

No camera can capture
All the beauty one sees
In a precious album
Of sweet memories!

by Virginia Glenham
1986

Memories

Memories are "mind-movies" from out of the past,
    One can put them on "hold" or "re-play"
To view when relaxed — and more wondrous still,
    To watch on your busiest day.

And now that the Christmas Season is here,
    The re-runs keep coming to view;
You're one of the stars — it's so pleasant for me
    To have such special memories of you!

by Virginia Glenham

The Years Tell Much

The years tell much that the days never knew.
   (The days didn't notice the change in pace
   'Til all of a sudden it's a different place.)
The town — now a city — just grew and grew.

The years tell much that the days didn't know.
   (The days were still very young in mind,
   But age has a way of creeping behind.)
Suddenly the wrinkles begin to show.

The years keep on going and are written down.
   (Birth, baptism, graduation,
   Marriage, children, war and inflation.)
The days were all buried under the ground.

   It seems it's the days that treat me well;
   It's the years that are such a tattletale!

by Virginia Glenham
1984

Disenchanted

When your husband has gone and you are alone
You're no longer a person, you're a statistic;
You're no longer accepted; couples are protected;
So you struggle to be realistic.

There's no one to need you; no one to heed you;
You must make a life of your own,
Pretend that it's rosy, comfortable, cozy,
But it's desolate, being alone.

If there is a time when you go out to dine
At a restaurant or cafeteria,
You can't help but eye all the couples nearby
And feel out-of-place or inferior.

I wonder why they don't seem happy and gay;
Do they take their lives so for granted?
They are so blessed, and I am distressed
That it's "they" who look disenchanted.

by Virginia Glenham
1986

Old Days, Old Friends

Where are the old days,
 The joyous, the fun days,
Where are the old days,
 The days of long ago?

They died with the Winters,
 The Autumns, the Summers,
They died with their season,
 The days of long ago.

Where are the old friends,
 The good friends, the true friends,
Where are the old friends
 We used to love and know?

Some died in their Summers,
 Some died in their Autumns,
Still living in memories,
 Dear friends of long ago.

by Virginia Glenham
1963

Friendship

How long is a friendship?
   Nobody knows -
It seems that our friendship
   Just grows and grows!

It's good to have
   It's silent assurance,
And to know in our hearts
   It's strong endurance.

How long is forever?
   Our friendship's that long;
To be shared in memories
   And on the wings of a song!

by Virginia Glenham
May, 1981

Warm Neighbors

The doors in this neighborhood are closed
    'Cause it's Wintertime, and a cold wind blows;
It seems that everyone wants to reside
    Near the warmth of a hearth-fire burning inside!

Soon the doors will fling open — when Spring comes around
    With it's green grass and flowers carpeting the ground;
The smiles and "hellos" will be heard far and wide,
    And the warmth will be felt from the hearts outside!

by Virginia Glenham

Waiting

Waiting for the rain to stop,
Waiting for the day to end,
Waiting for dinner to be served,
Waiting for meaning to begin;
Waiting for Spring or Summer,
Waiting for Winter or Fall,
Waiting for a commercial to finish,
Waiting for someone to call;
Waiting for a vacation,
Waiting for Christmas to come,
Waiting for payday or Sunday,
Waiting for time to go home;
Seems like I'm always waiting
No matter how busy the day,
Just waiting to start waiting
For what I'm going to say;
Waiting for things to get better,
Waiting for things to get worse,
Waiting for someone to stop me
From trying to finish this verse!

by Virginia Glenham — 1985

On Retiring

There must be better ways to see the sunset
Than stalling in traffic, waiting for lights;
There are beautiful rivers I'm wanting to cross;
There are mountains and valleys and breathtaking sights.

As I pack up my things, I'll take bits of you
To store in my mind and in my heart's treasure;
I'll take them out in the days to come
And reflect on each one with love and with pleasure!

by Virginia Glenham
December, 1980

Belated Birthday

I let your birthday slip by me
    But when I look at you
You look so young — it makes me know
    Some must have skipped you, too.

by Virginia Glenham

Longevity

I just couldn't let the day go by
    Without saying the inevitable;
People who have the most birthdays
    Live the longest —
        Ain't that incredible?

by Virginia Glenham

Our Pastor

Our pastor's greatest sermon
   Is the one he lives each day;
It's full of love and giving
   Because he lives this way.

It comes from his parents' teachings,
   It comes from God's Holy Word,
It comes from majestic music,
   The sweetest ever heard.

Compassion is always in it,
   The joy of living, too;
It shows how to be happy
   With values that are true.

Yes, our pastor's greatest sermon
   Is the one he lives each day;
For God reveals Himself through him
   In His Own Inimitable Way!

by Virginia Glenham
May, 1985

To My Doctor

If happiness is in caring for others,
You should be the happiest person I know;
You restore to your patients their dignity
When often their spirits are low.

You make one feel like a real person,
That life means a lot after all;
You are head and shoulders above all the rest,
In my heart you are ten feet tall!

by Virginia Glenham

Senior Citizen Quiz

Who am I?
Why am I here?
The best years of my life have passed;
Many loved ones and friends
No longer are near.
Why should I be the last?

The days are so lonely
And nights move so slowly
There's little that I can still do
Except to watch
Great grandchildren grow
And bring out old memories to view.

But I can still hear
And I can still see,
In some ways I truly am blessed;
My Heavenly Father
Is caring for me.
So why am I ever distressed?

Who am I?
Why am I here?
Each life has it's change of season;
As long as I live
I have nothing to fear;
My Lord has His own perfect reason.

by Virginia B. Glenham

SHADOWS

of

From My Heart

Then and Now

When we first moved into this little home
    Nearly fifty years ago,
Across the street were stalks of corn
    Standing stately in a row.

In the evening we'd sit on this little clean porch
    Which was noticeably bare,
Except for the steps and the stoops on each side
    And an old wooden rocking chair.

Sometimes dad would play his harmonica
    A sweet and plaintive tune
To the background of crickets chirping
    — The only light was fireflies and moon.

(Now — the porch has swings on either side
    But it still is noticeably bare,
For no longer is it filled with children
    And their laughter in the air.)

I can still remember the games we played,
    The happiness that was theirs,
The bandaging up of bruises
    From their jumping down the stairs.

The yard seemed so much larger then
    For baseball games and such,
And grass never had time to grow
    But we didn't mind that much.

More ...

(Now — the grass is green — there's shrubbery, too;
    Pretty flowers have been sown,
But it doesn't have any meaning
    As I sit here all alone.)

Now — houses are all around me.
    Many neighbors have come and gone,
And there are no children to play in the street
    Since all of them have grown.

The quiet is almost deafening,
    And as the day is done,
I find myself dreading to go inside
    To set the table for one.

Even though the children are far away
    And have families of their own,
I hear them say, "When I turn down this street,
    I know I am coming home!"

by Virginia Glenham

Making Memories

How often, during the span of a day
My mind settles back to enjoy a re-play —
    Flash-backs in memory of the good times we've had;
    (Can't seem to remember if any were bad.)
A little click — and all of the children are young again,
Turn on the sound — and our songs will be sung again!

It's so exciting — I can't ever be blue,
'Cause evenings and weekends I'm home with you
    With a whole new setting — a plot to unveil
    Same old characters with a new story to tell.

(When you think about it — we've so much to do!
— Preparing new memories for tomorrow — to view!)

by Virginia Glenham

A Prayer

Dear Lord,

Long years ago
We gave our children to You,
And You're always there to watch over them
In all they think and do.

You've given them spouses who balance their lives
In their work and in their home;
They all know You and turn to You;
They know they are never alone.

I thank You for the privilege
Of letting us share in each life;
For the joys of sharing their growing years,
Yes, even for hurts and for strife.
     They needed the hard times to make them strong;
     They needed the faith that brought them along.

I thank You for their love
And the things they achieve,
And most of all — for You, Lord,
In Whom they believe!

by Virginia Glenham
February, 1987

51

I and Me

She always said "me" instead of "I"
And 'twas time to be starting to school,
So we corrected and cautioned and struggled to teach
Which "me" or "I" was the rule.

And then one morning she got it right;
When her father came home she was ready;
As I praised her accomplishment, she hastily cried,
"I didn't know me could say that — did you, daddy!"

by Virginia Glenham
August, 1987

The Teddy Bear

I wish I hadn't done it —
Tho 'twas many years ago;
My little son was to look the best,
But how was I to know?

All his class were to dress like Christmas toys,
And he, a teddy bear;
For him to look more realistic
Was my every thought and care.

I cut his teddy bear's head for a mask
So he could play the part,
But I didn't know until too late
I had cut out a piece of his heart.

by Virginia Glenham
August, 1987

My Father

"Let me stay up just five minutes more,"
As a child to my father I'd say;
The next thing I knew, in my drowsy sleep
His strong arms were lifting away.
How I'd love to feel once more that secure,
So sure of his love and his care;
No worries, no troubles, just bright aimless days
And contentment that daddy would always be there.
(There were years when I thought I was wiser than he;
Now I find it's his wisdom that is uplifting to me!)

by Virginia Glenham

I Love You, Mom

"I love you, Mom; Now you take care."
The sweetest words to a mother's ear
When children go so far away
And on the phone you hear them say,
        "I love you, Mom; Now you take care!"

Seems only a little while ago
That off to school or work they'd go
'Twas quiet, once you closed the door,
But wasn't very long before
        You heard, "Hey, Mom, I'm here!"

Now, they have their lives and I have mine;
'Tis a tranquil life most of the time;
But oh, how sweetly my heart sings
When suddenly the telephone rings
        And I hear, "I love you, Mom — take care!"

by Virginia Glenham
1986

Big Brother

Twenty-seven years ago,
The thirtieth of November,
God gave to us a little son!
How well do we remember!
    And it may have rained,
    Or it may have snowed,
    Or it may have been bright and clear;
But the memory that lingers in our hearts
Was — a little son is here!

Dad was so proud — he cried out loud —
What, with two daughters before you —
And all of us made such a fuss!
And we all do still adore you!
    Since then — two more sons —
    How rich we are!
    Five children, a Dad, and a Mother —
But if you only knew — and it's so true —
We all look up to Big Brother.

by Virginia Glenham

Forty

"Forty" sounds so young to me —
    Seems only yesterday,
I saw you as you left for school,
    And watched you run and play.

The yard seemed so much larger then
    For the house where grass never grew,
What with baseball games and kites and such
    And the neighbors kids you knew!

And now you have sons of your own;
    You are so much like your dad,
Giving them both an abundance of love
    And things you never had.

Yes, life is rich when you know that God
    Is with you every minute.
So live gently — one day at a time —
    Inhale the joy that's in it.

Someday your sons will be forty
    And you can smile and say,
"Forty sounds so young to me —
    Seems only yesterday ..."

by Virginia Glenham

Just Like Her Mother

The day she was born they brought her to me,
The sweetest little baby I ever did see!
And when she primped up her face and started to cry,
Dad winked at the nurse who was standing by
    And said, "She looks just like her mother!"

She mimicked me in her formative years,
She laughed when I laughed, and we shed mingled tears;
It soon became quite evident —
She took after me — wherever I went!
    Yes, she took after her mother!

It seems the years have literally flown
Now she has a daughter of her own
And she understands how it was with me —
All those days that used to be,
    And her daughter takes after her mother!

Once in a while when the telephone rings,
An anxious voice asks me how I do things —
And my heart skipped a beat when I overheard her say
(The same way I feel about my mother today)
    "I wish I were more like MY MOTHER!"

by Virginia Glenham
April, 1981

First Daughter

You went through a period of "expectancy"
— and then came the feeling of "ecstacy"
Having the thrill that, of course, you oughta
When the doctor said, "You've a baby daughter!"

A tiny little bundle
And suddenly you realize
This precious little doll is real —
She breathes — she sleeps — AND SHE CRIES!

At first, she's just to coddle and love,
But the shock that brings on the dizziness
Is the realization that raising this child
Is what is known as BIG BUSINESS!

Everything you do — everywhere you go —
She's crawling — and she'll follow;
You have to vacuum as fast as you can
Or the "leap-jeeps" she will swallow!

She has a way that's all her own —
She's cunning and "all-knowing;"
It never fails — the pride that swells
When she models Grandma's sewing.

She can spill your powder — waste your perfume,
But you might as well forget it
Her dad will say it's all your fault —
You should place it where she can't get it!

More ...

Your frustrations can reach a danger point —
The very worst — I betcha,
Is when she needs a little switch —
If only you could catch her!

Oh, the Holidays! — the First Day of School —
All become special occasions —
The sweet memories of her growing up —
The lively family vacations!

Her Confirmation — Her Graduation —
And then, too soon, she's grown;
She finds the young man she loves the most —
She has a little girl of her own!

As a baby, a tot, a teenager, a wife —
A daughter's a dear — she's a blessing for life.

And it's great to pick up the telephone
And hear her saying, "I'm glad you're home —
How do you do this — or how do you make that?
How pleasant — this Mother-Daughter chat!

And it never matters just how you're greeted —
The JOY is knowing that you're still needed!

by Virginia Glenham

To Tony
(Christmas, 1979)

A special thoughtwave to Heaven —
    I'm sure 'twill find you there;
A special thoughtwave to Heaven —
    To tell you that I care!

It's Christmastime and everyone is joyful
    With presents underneath the Christmas tree,
It's obvious that two of them are missing —
    Mine for you — and yours for me,

A special thoughtwave to Heaven —
    A royal celebration where!
I hope someday to be invited
    To come and join you there.

by Virginia Glenham

To Tony
(Valentine, 1980)

In my memory window grows a Valentine tree
It holds all the ones we gave to each other;
Each heart, each verse from you and from me
Will continue to blossom forever.

I still feel your love although you are gone,
And I'm filled with loss and with longing;
But our love will continue to go on and on
With the sureness one has in belonging.

One more blossom to add to the tree —
I'll hang it, pretending it's yours to me!

by Virginia Glenham

To My Husband

Honey, if you can hear me,
Were you with me today?
Did you see all our family together
In such a delightful way?
You see, they all surprised me
Because I have just retired,
And each has a personality
So greatly to be admired!
Did you hear how they talked about us —
Times when they were still at home?
Do you see how well they are doing
In the homes that are their own?
The grandchildren, too, are growing up
So talented, beautiful, too;
And to think such a loving family
Started with me and you!
Honey, if you can hear me,
Let's thank God for this special day
For He's always showing His love for us all
In His Own Inimitable Way!

by Virginia Glenham
June 29, 1986

Marie

The Lord sent an angel
    To live on the earth
To be a blessing to many
    From her moment of birth.

She was fashioned with beauty;
    With a song in her heart,
With a passion for living
    And God's Love to impart.

This love was contagious
    A true epidemic
Which spread through her life
    To everyone in it.

Her loved ones, so precious
    Her friends were her treasure,
To all whom she knew
    She gave beyond measure.

Suddenly our Lord
    Called this angel home;
To the glory of Heaven
    Our angel has flown.

Her legacy to us is
    That when you're in prayer
You'll know the presence
    Of our Father is there;
And if you hear with your heart
    As the choir sings,
You may feel the brush
    Of an angel's wings!

by Virginia B. Glenham

It's Just Me — Tonda

She was always thinking of others,
    Concerned with each need and care;
Surely God created her
    An angel unaware
For she never felt she was worthy
    When love to her was shown;
Her humility was astounding
    And only to God was known.
        When she called me on the phone each day,
        In her soft, sweet voice I would hear her say,
        "Mom, it's just me — Tonda."

She always honored her parents
    And when she became a wife
Her husband and two daughters
    Brought fulfillment to her life.
Her sister and her brothers, too
    Held a special place in her heart
And always uppermost in her mind
    God played a major part.
        When she faces Him I can just hear her say
        In her soft and sweet and humble way,
        "Lord, it's just me — Tonda."

by Virginia Glenham
December, 1989

(Written for my daughter, Tonda Aquino, age 43,
who died December 21, 1989 with leukemia.)

Dad at Christmas

Dad always loved Christmas —
How he'd polish the floors,
Find just the right tree
To bring pine scent indoors;

He loved holly and mistletoe,
Everyone singing
All the old carols —
He loved the bells ringing.

The house had aromas
Of Christmas ham baking,
Of candles burning,
Of cakes in the making.

The Candlelight Service
To him meant so much;
Felt it couldn't be held
Without his special touch.

He loved giving presents
That would be a surprise,
And the gifts he received
Brought tears to his eyes.

He thought of Christmas
As a time for sharing,
Thinking of others
By doing and caring.

Christmas meant visiting
And helping the poor,
Welcoming everyone
Who came to our door.

More ...

Enjoying the children,
Loving each minute
Of what Christmastime means
And all the joys in it!

And the tree stayed up
Until New Year's Day;
To take it down sooner
Was bad luck, he would say.

It's good — laughing and loving —
Reliving the past
In pleasant remembrances
That were born to last;

And life still goes on
Pretty much as before,
For traditions passed down
Are too hard to ignore.

Someday the grandchildren
Will be grams or grand-dads
Carrying on the traditions
All of us had;

And although we can't see him,
Dad's presence is here
Enjoying this day
       — and each day of the year.

by Virginia Glenham
June, 1987

Hand-Me-Down

Three sons ago this shirt was new —
     Button-down collar and tapered line
I wonder if 'twill seem like new
     To son — age nine.

by Virginia Glenham
September, 1965

Southern Childhood Memory

Long summer days and peaceful nights,
Sitting on porches in rocking chairs
Talking across to the neighbors next door,
Breakfast, dinner, supper, and saying our prayers.

Minstrels standing on the corner to sing,
Dad sending a dime for a special tune;
Children playing games like "Kick the Can",
Lovers making wishes on the new moon.

Crickets at twilight, birds in the morning,
Dad coming home when the day was done;
Storms that came up without any warning,
Spring cleaning with mattresses outside in the sun.

Couldn't go barefoot until May,
Vicks on chest and covered with flannel,
Open fireplace with it's dancing flames,
An old chiming clock high up on the mantel.

Cousins coming from ten miles away
Bringing vegetables and fruit they had grown,
Telling ghost stories with spine chilling sounds
'Bout graveyards and witches and all the unknown.

Chewing licorice from licorice trees
Pretending your mouth was juicy with snuff,
Cocoa and sugar looked mostly the same
But tasted so good — 'twas never enough.

More ...

Sticking wild onion stems into a hole,
Telling the Doodle-bug it's house was on fire,
Then jerking it out so that it could see
That it's curious tormenter was really a liar.

Never missed going to church on Sunday,
Polishing shoes the night before,
Going to sleep on my father's shoulder
 Because the sermon was such a bore.

Bible verses and hymns I learned as a child
May seem to be hidden away,
But they rise to the surface in time of need
With comfort and strength for the day.

While life is easier than in days long ago,
More money, more time, and more luxury,
I feel far richer than others I know
With my southern childhood memory.

by Virginia Glenham

SHADOWS

of

The War Years

Lost Time

I Dreaded War

I dreaded war until last night
Because you'd have to go,
I thought I'd never give you up
To go where bugles blow.
My soul was swelled with hatred
Of the patriotic veins
That flow through young men's bodies
And leave but bloody stains.
I'd pictured a thousand war scenes,
I'd seen our soldiers die,
I'd seen young widowed mothers,
Sweethearts and children cry.
My bitterness possessed me,
I raised my head and swore
That I would rather go to hell
Than live through a bitter war.
But somehow last night changed me;
Something in your eyes
Made me feel a glory
In the far-off battlecries.

by Virginia Glenham
1941

To My Soldier Sweetheart

Fight, my soldier sweetheart, raise your gun,
Be sure and steady with your deadly aim,
And I will hear it's blast — I'll see it's flame,
I'll feel each shot until the war is done.
And when you try to sleep at night I'll come
And take your head and hold it to my breast,
I'll sing to you until I know you rest,
And wake with you before the rising sun.

And oh, my soldier sweetheart I'll be true,
I'll count each minute 'til you come to me
When the war is over and we've won
We'll pretend our lives have just begun!
But — what if you should die (this cannot be!)
Then, darling, wait and I will come to you.

by Virginia Glenham
1942

I Am Your Wife

Could I but hold your head tonight upon my breast,
    Could I but stroke your hair, or clasp your hand;
How much I love you, even you have never guessed,
    But oh, my dear, I know you understand.

What price we pay for the love we share,
    What price we would pay to be together,
But come what may, what do we care;
    Our love will stand the storms we weather.

Our love will live because it is so true,
    So deep, so great — even greater than life;
And as I close my eyes, I think of you,
    And oh, I thank my God I am your wife.

by Virginia Glenham
1943

You Are Asleep

You are asleep
But I don't mind;
My thoughts run deep
When you're asleep
Of secret joys I love to keep;
I steal a kiss and then I find
You are asleep
But I don't mind.

by Virginia Glenham
1945

71

All The Things You Are

You are to me the early morning light
That floods my room and opens up my eyes,
A new beginning everyday before me lies
And fills my heart with wondering delight.
My mind's eye keeps you evermore in sight
And every beauty I compare with you;
You're everything that's real and good and true,
You're everything for which I'd ever fight.

I hear a magic chord and think of you;
The harmony breaks my heart, it is so sweet;
I read a lovely poem and you're there, too;
I am forever kneeling at your feet.
My wants and wishes in this life are few,
As long as I have you — my world's complete.

by Virginia Glenham
1942

My Love For You

I try to think of words — they are not there,
Those hidden words that tell my love for you;
My love is great and deep and true —
Those words seem little written here.
Above all else in life you are so dear,
To look at you can take my heart away,
You have the power to turn my night to day,
Your loving presence drowns my every fear.

I try and try and yet no words can show
Because I have your love makes life devine;
Our love has, like a torch, a burning glow
That will not dim and will forever shine;
But deep within my heart I know you know —
I've always felt your love — you must feel mine!

by Virginia Glenham
1943

I Haven't Time

I haven't time to think of clouds;
  My man has gone to war
And I must stay and make a home
  That is worth his fighting for.

Don't ask me if I see the moon
  Or thrill at nature's ways;
I watch my children grow by nights,
  I earn our bread by days.

And Spring will not mean love this year,
  I shall not see the flowers bloom,
My heart is full of sweat and toil,
  For else there is no room.

I haven't time to think of clouds;
  My man has gone to war
And I must stay and make a home
  That is worth his fighting for.

by Virginia Glenham
1944

If I Should Live

If I should live a thousand years
     My love for you would never change;
Our moments brief, our laughs, our tears
     Live young in memories, never growing strange.

You are so much a part of me,
     With you away — I always find you near
Somehow. I only have to think
     How very sweet you are and dear.

I hear your thoughts like little whispers
     When I need you most. It seems
As though a winged angel joins our hearts
     And keeps us close in dreams.

Let time sweep by, let ages pass
     And matter not how long the time appears,
My love for you will outlast
     A hundred, thousand, million years.

by Virginia Glenham
1945

Beautiful Times

It's easy to remember the beautiful times,
But to re-live them would be a disaster
For they were submerged in war's dark troubled times
     And it's only the beauty I'm after!

by Virginia Glenham

Let Him Know

I see him now, his eyes so bright,
His fair head gleaming in the sun
Like a halo, and he said,
"I'll be back when we are done."
"When we are done," how light he said it,
So consoling and so sure
That even I could see soon victory
And our homes again secure.

And now he's gone — gone with the halo
Up above the sun,
And so, God, when this war is over,
Let him know 'twas our side won.

by Virginia Glenham
1943

Every Way I Turn

Every way I turn I see your face before me,
Every way I turn I feel you there,
Every song of love rings out how you adore me,
Every way I turn I know you care.

So many memories —
Keep flashing through my mind,
And all the troubled times
Seem now so hard to find.

Every way I turn you are my inspiration
All the loving dreams we used to share,
And now it seems my only consolation
Is knowing that someday you'll turn and I'll be there!

by Virginia Glenham
April, 1979

Wake Me Up, Lord

Wake me up, Lord, when it's over;
    Let me sleep 'til it is done;
It's so hard to keep on living
    'Tween the rise and set of sun.

My heart is broken, blood is seeping,
    Pain is more than I can bear;
And my eyes are filled with weeping;
    Please, Lord, take me in Your care.

Help me to accept this sorrow,
    Not judge others for it's cause;
Let there be a healed tomorrow,
    Free my mind from all it's flaws.

Only You, Lord, know the suffering,
    Know it's depth, the hurt, the pain;
Hold me close, Lord, 'til it's over;
    Let me want to live again.

by Virginia Glenham
January, 1989

SHADOWS

of

Young Love

Dreams and Things

The Day You Didn't Write

I thought I wouldn't miss you,
    That things would be all right,
But, oh, my heart was broken —
    The day you didn't write.

That I didn't love you
    I told myself for spite
Just to hide my wounded pride
    The day you didn't write.

But I was so mistaken
    To think I didn't care,
And my heart started breaking
    The day I met the postman — and your
        letter wasn't there!

And now that you are here again
    I must confess tonight,
I realized I loved you then —
    The day you didn't write.

by Virginia Glenham

I Used To Love With Laughter

I used to love with laughter and songs of the stars and the moon;
At night you'd come and after — the dawn would come too soon

Oh, I loved the wind and the birds and the trees,
I loved the rainy days too,
I loved everybody because the somebody
I really loved was you!

But now I love with a broken heart, with the ache of unshed tears
And night can never come too soon, nor pass too fast the years.

I still love the wind and the birds and the trees
I love the rainy days too;
They make me sad — but still I'm glad
Because they remind me of you!

by Virginia Glenham
1939

A Woman's Love

You say you love me more than I love you
But, darling, can't you see you're vain?
A woman's love is far more true;
A man's love only causes pain.

A year from now you'll have forgot
The ecstacy we shared today;
Ten years from now I'll think of you
And wonder why you went away.

by Virginia Glenham

Maybe

Maybe I'll forget you,
At least I'll surely try;
Maybe I'll forget you,
(Oh, heart, you mustn't cry!)
Maybe I'll forget you,
It seems impossible now,
But maybe I'll forget you
Some day, somewhere, somehow.

by Virginia Glenham

Young Love

You are so young
You do not know what true love is —
You are so young,
For you the moon above
Has just begun;
To you the cooing dove
A song has sung.
Ah, me — you are so young!

by Virginia Glenham
1938

SHADOWS

of

School Days

Flickering Shadows

Adolescence

All the hardness of a maiden,
All the bitterness of living,
All that dwells in hearts of cynics
    Comes upon a girl at eighteen.

She who loved so pure and freely,
She who conquered hearts of young men,
She who found but disappointment
    Trusts her youthful heart to no one.

Once she trusted so completely
Everyone who offered friendship,
But that trust is gone at eighteen;
    She becomes a sage of wisdom.

But perhaps when she is twenty
She will then resume her sweetness;
Souvenirs of life she'll treasure,
    Smile through tears and love will welcome.

by Virginia Glenham
1936

Cinquains

I
The man
Up in the moon
Is my ideal, but since
I cannot go to him, I'll stay
With you.

II
Your words
Are like a little
Golden arrow, speeding
From Cupid's fatal bow
    to wound
My heart.

III
My thoughts
Today are like
The ripples on the sea;
They start and spread
    with sparkling
Memories.

Tercet
Fate is a mighty witch
Who weaves my life in which
She intentionally drops
    a stitch.

by Virginia Glenham
1937

87

Sonnet

Oh let me take you far away from here,
Away from home and friends and all the things
That do not understand us now, and cling
To all the dreams that we have held so dear;
And dance to music you and I alone can hear.
They do not like you so they hate me, too
Because I am so very much in love with you;
Oh let me take you far away from here.

We would come back a thousand years from now
And prove to them that they were very wrong;
I'd pour my priceless treasure at their feet
And say that life with you was full and sweet;
My treasure would consist of one love song —
But still they would not understand, somehow.

by Virginia Glenham
1938

Not Dead But Forgotten

I was searching vainly the other night in my chest of souvenirs
To find a little trinket that so often brings me tears.
It was given me by a person whom I thought my dearest
   friend
Until fate changed direction and made our friendship end.
We once walked side by side in every activity at school,
And we played jokes on each other, especially on April's Fool.
This little trinket was a ring he'd given me on this day;
He had hidden it in some candy, but there it didn't stay;
For when I bit into the piece, I took the ring away
And placed it with my souvenirs, and there it will always stay.
But I was just another girl to the giver of that ring,
And I admit that now and then I do a foolish thing;
I put this gift into a box and took a little glue
And pasted on it his picture, inscribed, "Not dead but fogotten
   by you."
And even now I wonder if our friendship really died;
Sometimes I feel we're playing that familiar game of "Hide".
So I look forward to the day that will bring us together again,
And when I think it might not come, there is a throb of pain
That strikes me like a weapon of the very deadliest kind.
I pray that in this game of "Hide" I'll have the luck to find!

by Virginia Glenham
1935

Teenager's Dream Home

Oh, Home, that is not yet more than a dream,
A dream that has a chance to coming true,
I hold the deeper things in life for you,
A home where firelight casts it's loving gleam;
A home where little children laugh or scream
In joy or in the sorrows that come due,
A home that welcomes weary travelers, too,
To come and share it's high or lowly means.

Your beauty counts but naught in looks, dear Home,
Though splendor mark each beam from which you're made,
'Tis not the concrete things in life that count;
Nor does money, no matter the amount,
'Tis love you can not get in books, dear Home,
That makes you "home," even after you've decayed.

by Virginia Glenham

Lost Youth

I weep for old houses — the "Homes" they used to be!
  What wondrous stories did they live?
  What laughter, love or tears did give?
  What bit to history did they sieve?
I weep for old houses — the "Homes" they used to be!

My heart cries when the whistle from a train sounds to my ears;
  What cargo now is theirs to hold?
  What stories have they left untold?
  Where are the passengers of old?
My heart cries when the whistle of a train sounds to my ears!

I long for the old friendships, and loves of yester-year.
  So many loved ones here no more —
  Nothing seems as it did before —
  My soul is sad and sick and sore;
I long for the old friendships, and loves of yester-year!

I grasp — and know I cannot bring back those wasted days.
  When I was young, they were so slow.
  Just when, and how did my children grow?
  Time now is fleeting — all I know .....
I grasp — and know I cannot bring back those wasted days.

by Virginia Glenham
April 27, 1965

Ecstatic Mood

I love the stars
    And the shadowy trees
That sway in time
    With the balmy breeze;
The night clouds that look
    Like dark fluffy wings
Lazily, weary — then a heavenly thing —
    The white Milky Way
With it's magic allure;
How much more beauty
Can my heart endure?
Orion was lucky to be thrown in such space;
Let me climb to the stars and take the moon's place!

by Virginia Glenham
1938

Life's Sunset

Before the evening darkens,
When the sun sinks in the sky,
While birds go flying homeward
And twilight still is nigh;
When the moon rises slowly
And stars shine one by one,
I think of a beautiful sunset
That some day will come;
When age sweeps o'er our bodies
And death knocks at our door,
Then Christ shall reign forever,
Yes, forever more.

by Virginia Glenham
1934

Life

Scarlet cloak
  On shoulders bending,
Traveling roads
  That have no ending,
Dreary skies
  Crying, weeping,
Lazy days
  Drowzily sleeping,
Golden sun
  Peeping through
Silver clouds
  In the blue,
Misery
  Lined with sorrow,
Mystery
  In tomorrow.
There he goes
  'Til the end
Blazing the trail
  For a friend.
Such is life!

by Virginia Glenham
1937

I've Wondered

How often have I wondered as I sit here all alone
If there is some deed of kindness that sometime I might have
done,
    And if there is,
    Is it still too late
    To perform that deed
    That's not out of date?

How often have I wondered, "Is there anything I can do?"
When I should go ahead and see, and help pull someone
through;
    And if I don't go,
    Will God reserve
    A star in my crown
    When I didn't serve?

And still I sometimes wonder, "What have I ever done?"
I believe I'll start life over, and then I'll help someone;
    But then I forget
    And sin again.
    Will I ever ride
    That heavenly train?

But if I ask the help of God to see me safely through,
And let me be a blessing in everything I do,
    I find life so much easier,
    I find deeds to be done,
    And when my life is over
    I'll know I've helped someone.

by Virginia Glenham
1934

Tomorrow I'll Escape

The Fates have had their way today,
Their schemes have all come true;
They've twisted and knotted the thread of my life,
They've completely cut out you!

But tomorrow I shall escape from their grasp,
I'll find that broken string,
And then while they're raveling some other life
I'll tie it together again.

by Virginia Glenham
1939

Life is slow,
   Life is fast,
      Life is present,
         Life is past,
            Life is in,
               Life is out;
                  Such is life
                     Without a doubt.

by Virginia Glenham
1936

The Great Coronation

I'm going to the coronation of a grand and glorious king,
Where trumpets will be sounded while the throngs of people sing,
And even the walls of Heaven will be one melodious ring!
      And a new world He will show me
      While the burdened world below me
Shall forever in the future be a forgotten thing.

I'm going to the coronation of the Savior of the World,
Upon whose blessed body many a stone was hurled,
And the thorns that pierced that head so beautifully curled
      Have pierced my heart with sorrow
      So that I long for the morrow
When my sins shall be all banished and His banner be unfurled.

And at the coronation of this wonderful King so great
The lives of all who hated Him will be turned o'er to fate;
That He shall reign forever, no one will debate
      For He shall have a kingdom
      Of liberty, of freedom
While the Heavenly Territory will be one eternal state.

No sorrow will be witnessed after my King is crowned;
No death, no sin, no evil thoughts will ever have a sound;
And happiness and peace will then spread all around
      While His subjects all sing
      "Long live our King!"
Then life everlasting will have been found.

by Virginia Glenham
1937

To A Tree

O wonderful tree
Silouetted against the sky,
You seem so real,
I wonder why
You can't talk to me
As I talk to you;
You'd have a keener
Story, 'tis true.
What secrets do you have
Concealed in your heart?
I'm sure you have one
Beneath your bark!
Perhaps some lovers
Have 'neath your boughs parted;
Was the scene happy,
Or were they broken-hearted?
How many birds
Have been in your protection?
Do they always come back
From the same direction?
I know the breeze loves you;
Even now it caresses
Your lofty branches
With soft kisses.
Why, you're so tall
You see everything!
You know the language
Of the birds that sing.
You understand the wind
As she whispers to you;
You keep lots of
Secrets, don't you?
I'd like to sit here
Awhile in your shade
And thank God once more
For the beauty He's made!

by Virginia Glenham
1935

Ladies' Hats

Men get blamed just lots of times
For various this's and that's,
But I wouldn't blame a man who'd strike
Because of ladies' hats!
They're the dinkiest things I ever saw —
The modern hats, I mean;
In spite of all the crazy shapes
Some people think they're keen.
Now there's a hat that's not a hat,
Just a band around the head;
Then there's a skull-like fitter
That one should wear when dead.
There's hats that go up in a peak,
And hats with bills like birds,
There's hats with veils and hats without;
"Dinky," "crazy" aren't the words
To describe the hats of the modern day —
They're positively "ignoramous,"
(I made up that word for my own use,
I hope it's like unanimous.)
I wonder if in the future,
Say, ten years from this fall,
If ladies will be buying invisible hats
That really aren't hats at all;
Like the emperor who wore no clothes
But he paid for them just the same.
If such a thing does come to pass,
'Twill surely be a shame
Though I wouldn't be a bit surprised
Cause at the modern rate
One simply has to buy ridiculous things
Just to be up-to-date.

by Virginia Glenham
1936

A Great Dancer

There was one time a maiden who loved to dance so well
That she danced from morn 'til evening so all the people tell
Until her parents thought her to their king they'd sell
　　'Cause she wanted to be a great dancer!

That this maiden was pretty no one could deny,
So the king when he saw her gave her a try;
She must dance without stopping three days or die,
　　And he'd make her then a great dancer!

So this maiden danced 'til her limbs they perspired;
One day she had danced and slowly she tired;
When she'd danced two days, the people all cried,
　　"She'll yet be a great dancer!"

The third day rolled by when her work would be done;
She danced on and on 'til the set of the sun;
Then she collapsed in the arms of the one
　　Who proclaimed her then a great dancer!

But her eyes never opened for she passed the ways,
Never witnessing the glory of the peoples' praise;
And this story they've handed down from those days
　　When she became a great dancer!

by Virginia Glenham
1936

Spur of the Moment Thought

If I could choose one of the following things:
      A million dollars,
      Pearls on a string,
      A world to rule,
      Youth without end,
      (And last, but not least,)
      A real true friend;
Perhaps I'd consider each one a bit,
And weigh the good and the counterfeit,
But I'm sure that richer I would be
With a real true friend — a friend to me.

by Virginia Glenham
1937

O Lika

      I lika da water,
      I lika da fish
      I lika da sailor,
      I lika ta wish
      Dat when I grow up
      I be de great whaler
      Dat catcha da fish
      Dat look lika sailor.

by Virginia Glenham

Unwritten Poem

I can't go to sleep;
A poem's on my mind;
I'm sure it's there
But it's so hard to find.
I almost had it
On the tip of my tongue;
It might be a song
That needs to be sung,
Or a masterpiece;
You never can tell;
'Twould be if I wrote it!
But, oh, ah well,
I am so sleepy
I can't scheme a bit.
Goodnight, maybe
I'll dream of it.

by Virginia Glenham
1942

I'd Like To Be ???

I'd like to be a toothpick,
A nice slim, graceful, toothpick,
So I could reach and touch your lips each day;
But no, that wouldn't do at all;
I might not be with you at all,
Or if I were, soon I'd be thrown away.

Oh, were I but a pencil,
A good-for-writing pencil,
Then I could feel the touch of your strong hand
I'd even be able to be of use,
Ah me, ah me, but what's the use?
You'd sharpen me 'til I'd be naught but sand!

Perhaps were I a necktie,
A very becoming necktie,
You might insist to wear me all the while;
Then I could be embracing you,
But soon I'd be disgracing you,
'Cause neckties, like all things, go out of style.

I guess I should be satisfied,
Though not one moment gratified,
To be the girl who thinks you're simply grand;
Then maybe fate will play my way
And make you come to me someday,
Then I can touch your lips, your neck, your hand.

by Virginia Glenham

Blowing Out The Light

'Twas the night after Christmas and time for retiring,
The kin folk were leaving — their time was expiring;
It had been a nice Christmas, their college boy home again,
But they couldn't help thinking they'd soon be alone again.
The wind outside sounded like the howl of a dog,
While the fire lay in embers of the last burning log.
Ma and Pa sat dozing — 'twas time for bed,
Sister Flossie was stretching and scratching her head;
The hired man was closing and bolting the door,
And the cat was snoring in a ball on the floor.
Ma said to Pa, "Pa, put the cat out,
And while you're doin' it — blow the lamp out."
Ma had forgotten Pa's mouth twisted to the right
And it was impossible for him to blow out the light.
"Ma, Ma, I can't blow it," he said when he tried,
So slowly but surely, she came to his side;
Just as she took a mighty deep breath,
She remembered her mouth twisted way to the left!
"Hey, Flossie, come 'ere," she hollered then,
Forgetting sis Flossie had a protruding chin;
No matter how hard she tried to blow
The lamp still burned with a steady glow.
Then she called the hired man — but his chin was receding,

More ...

He tried to blow the light out —

    but, of course, not succeeding.

Then the college son looked up in disgust,

And with great force of effort,

    thought he would do what he must;

He went to the lamp and bended just so

And blew the light out with one little blow!

Ma looked at Pa, and Pa looked at Ma,

Sis looked at the hired man and said, "Aw shaw!"

Now this might sound like a big fabrication —

But goes to show the value

Of a college education!

A skit put into verse,
by Virginia Glenham

SHADOWS

of

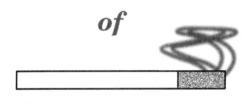

cigarettes

Lights Out!

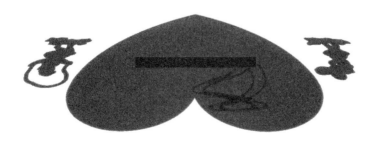

Trying To Quit

There is a lady distressed,
'Cause with cigarettes she is obsessed;
   Now she's wearing some patches,
   'Stead of cigarettes and matches,
To stop smoking she's doing her best.

*   *   *

Smoking is not attractive;
   It even gives bad breath;
      But the simple, awful fact is
         You can smoke yourself to death.

*   *   *

While I may be gaining a little weight,
My spirits are so much brighter;
For every cigarette I don't smoke,
I become a cigarette lighter.

*   *   *

If I keep right on smoking
   — which is often,
I know that I'll be paying
   — for my coughin'. (coffin)

by Virginia Glenham

Talking To Myself

Try to think of something funny,
Think of things to do,
Christmas Eve and Easter bunny,
Mardi Gras or Timbuktu;
Read the market, read Dear Abby,
Read the Bible — it's begats;
But ignore that broken record
That keeps playing, "Cigarettes...

Cigarettes...
        Cigarettes...
                Cigarettes..."

by Virginia Glenham
August 12, 1989

I'm trying to stop smoking
And I'm certainly not joking

When I say that it's the hardest thing to do;
        But my doctor's sympathetic
        And my nurse so anesthetic
That I'm quitting just for them (...and for me, too!)

by Virginia Glenham

I told Satan to get behind me
'Cause I wanted to do what's right,
But then I reached for a cigarette
And he gave me a light!

by Virginia Glenham
August 6, 1989

Cigarette "Butts"

I'd like to quit smoking ....

But   I'll wait another day;
But   Stresses get in the way;
But   I'm more sociable when smoking;
But   I'm more relaxed and joking;
But   Life seems far too gloomy;
But   I like to smoke — so sue me;

There are more "buts" than I can say,

Pardon me, while I empty this tray.

I'd like to keep on smoking ....

But   I'm feeling friendless and shunned;
But   My clothes have holes where they're burned;
But   My limited income is dwindling;
But   Vending machine are so swindling;
But   This continuous coughing is getting me down;
But   I feel I'm the last smoker left in this town;
But   If I want to smoke I must go into hiding;
But   There's no smoker left that I can confide in;
But   I know that smoking can shorten my days;
And that I'm the loser in this out-styled craze;

One more thing I'd like to explain,

But   The ashtray is filled with "buts" again;

It's "Ashes to ashes" — an adage so true,

That is what smoking can do for you ...... and me!

By Virginia Glenham
September, 1989